FERDINAND BEYER

VORSCHULE IM KLAVIERSPIEL
ELEMENTARY METHOD FOR PIANO

Opus 101

Herausgegeben von / Edited by

Adolf Ruthardt

EDITION PETERS
LEIPZIG · LONDON · NEW YORK

Vorwort

Vorliegendes Werk hat den Zweck, den angehenden Klavierspieler auf die möglich leichteste Weise in die schöne Kunst des Klavierspieles einzuführen.

Es ist dasselbe für Kinder, selbst des zartesten Alters, berechnet, und daher der Stufengang, ohne das Werk zu umfangreich zu machen, so fortschreitend als möglich gehalten worden. Daß eine erschöpfende Ausarbeitung aller im Klavierspiel vorkommenden Schwierigkeiten, sowie der Verzierungen u. s. w. nicht im Zwecke dieses Werkes liegen konnte, wird man nach dem Gesagten zugeben müssen.

Es sollte in der Tat nur eine Vorschule in den Anfangsgründen sein, welche dem Schüler während des ersten, vielleicht auch des zweiten Jahres hinlänglichen Stoff zur Tätigkeit darbietet.

An solchen Werken dürfte wohl bis jetzt Mangel sein und es kann dasselbe selbst musikalischen Eltern als Leitfaden dienen, das Kind für den Unterricht des Lehrers vorzubereiten.

Preface

The object of this work is to furnish young players with as easy an introduction as possible to the art of playing on the pianoforte.

It is intended for children, even of the tenderest age, and the progression has therefore been made as gradual as possible within the limits of the work. From this it will be clear that an exhaustive treatment of all the difficulties, ornaments, &c., does not lie within the scope of this book, which is not meant to be more than an elementary instruction book to furnish the pupil with material for practice during his first and perhaps second year.

There is, it is believed, room for a work of this kind which may also be used by musical parents in preparing their children for the professional master.

Préface

Le but du présent ouvrage est d'enseigner de la manière la plus facile le bel art du piano aux jeunes commençants.

Destiné aux enfants, même à ceux de l'âge le plus tendre, ce petit ouvrage devait être gradué aussi rigoureusement que possible sans atteindre pourtant une trop grande étendue. Après cet avertissement, on comprendra, je pense, qu'un traité complet et approfondi sur toutes les difficultés que présente le jeu du piano, ainsi que sur les ornements, etc., n'a pu entrer dans le plan de cet abrégé.

Ce n'est en effet qu'une simple introduction aux exercices préliminaires qui offriront à l'élève un élément de travail suffisant pendant la première et peut-être même pendant la deuxième année d'étude.

Le besoin d'oeuvres de ce genre se fait encore sentir de nos jours et le présent ouvrage peut aussi servir de guide aux parents musiciens pour instruire l'enfant depuis l'âge le plus tendre jusqu'à ce qu'il puisse être confié aux soins d'un professeur.

Ferdinand Beyer

Contents

First Stage
Page

Second Stage

Appendix

Table des Matières

Premier Degré
Page

Second Degré

Supplément

Anfangsgründe für die Klavierspieler | Elements of Music | Principes de musique à l'usage des élèves de piano

Notensystem
Stave
Portée

Linien
Lines
Lignes

Zwischenräume
Spaces
Interlignes

Hilfslinien
Ledger lines
Lignes supplémentaires

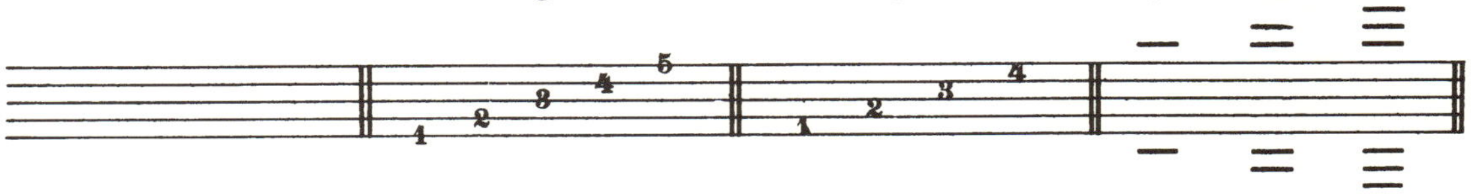
1 2 3 4 5
1 2 3 4

Violin-oder G-Schlüssel
Treble Clef
Clef de sol

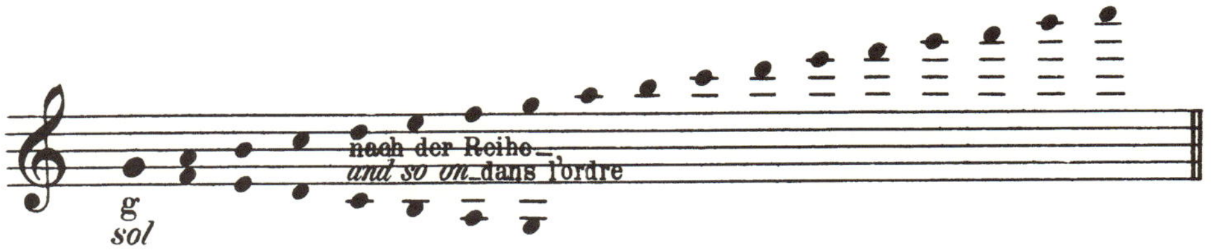
nach der Reihe
and so on dans l'ordre
g
sol

Baß- oder F-Schlüssel
Bass Clef
Clef de fa

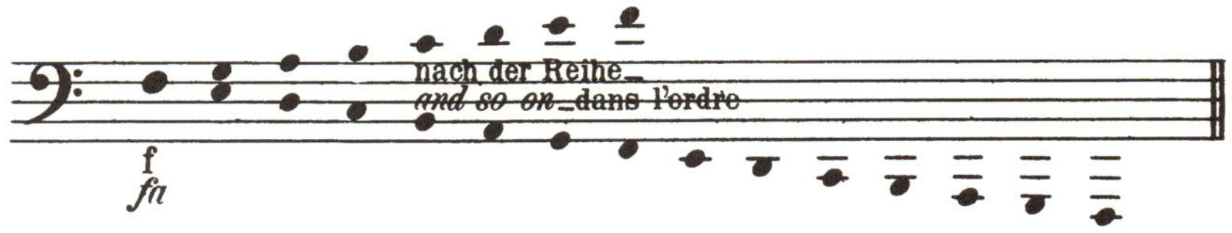
nach der Reihe
and so on dans l'ordre
f
fa

Noten auf den 5 Linien
Notes on the 5 lines
Notes sur les cinq lignes

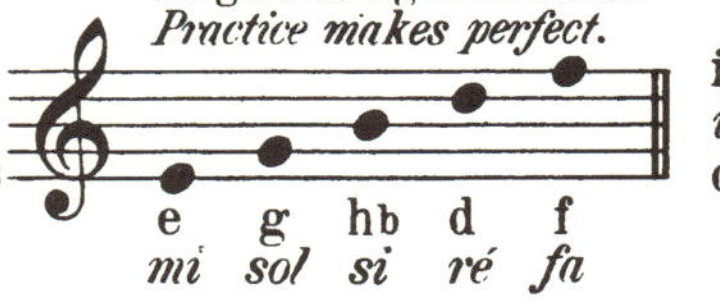
Es geht hurtig durch Fleiß.
Practice makes perfect.
e g hb d f
mi sol si ré fa

in den 4 Zwischenräumen
in the 4 spaces
dans les 4 interlignes

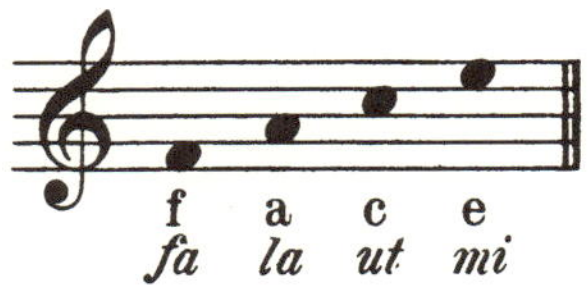
f a c e
fa la ut mi

Über und unter dem System
Above and below the stave
Au-dessus et au-dessous de la portée

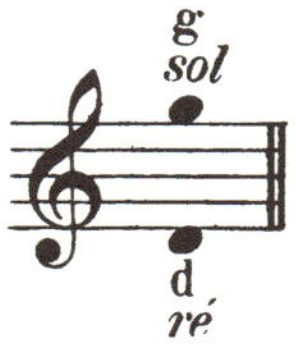
g
sol
d
ré

auf den Hilfslinien
on the ledger lines
sur les lignes supplémentaires

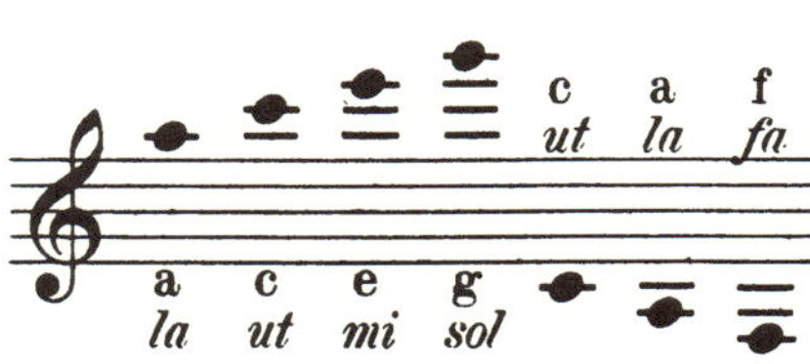
c a f
ut la fa
a c e g
la ut mi sol

Über und unter den Hilfslinien
Above and below the ledger lines
Au-dessus et au-dessous des lignes supplément

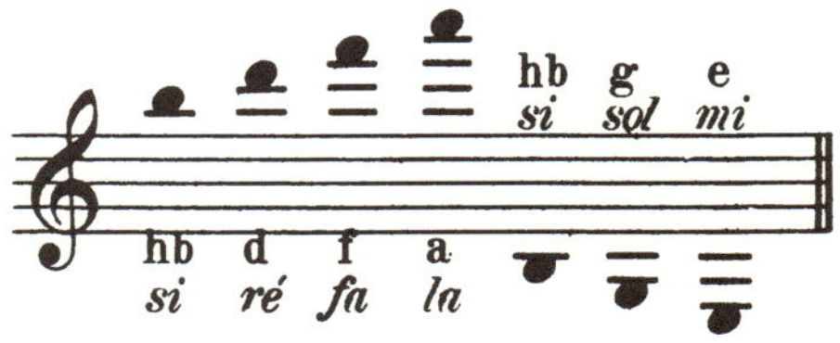
hb g e
si sol mi
hb d f a
si ré fa la

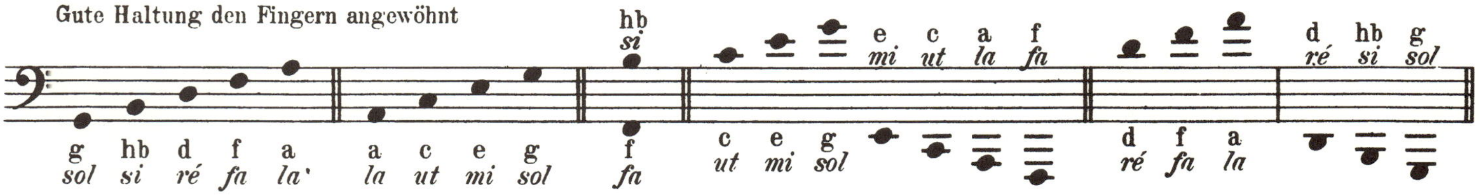
Gute Haltung den Fingern angewöhnt
g hb d f a
sol si ré fa la
a c e g
la ut mi sol
hb
si
f
fa
e c a f
mi ut la fa
c e g
ut mi sol
d f a
ré fa la
d hb g
ré si sol

Zur leichten Erlernung der Noten muß der Schüler das musikalische Alphabet: *c d e f g a h,* nach der Reihe und nach Terzenschritten: *c e g h d f a c,* vorwärts und rückwärts geläufig hersagen lernen und dies auf die Tasten und die Noten anwenden

To facilitate the learning of the notes the pupil must learn to repeat the musical alphabet fluently in succession: c d e f g a b, *and in thirds:* c e g b d f a c, *forwards and backwards, and to apply this to the keys and notes*

Pour apprendre facilement les notes, l'élève doit savoir couramment la gamme musicale: *ut ré mi fa sol la si,* d'abord dans l'ordre successif, puis en tierces: *ut mi sol si ré fa la ut,* en montant comme en descendant et l'appliquer aux touches et aux notes

Sekunde / *Seconds* / Seconde — Terz / *Thirds* / Tierce — Quarte / *Fourths* / Quarte — Quinte / *Fifths* / Quinte — Sexte / *Sixths* / Sixte — Septime / *Sevenths* / Septième — Oktave / *Octave* / Octave

Intervalle
Intervals
Intervalles

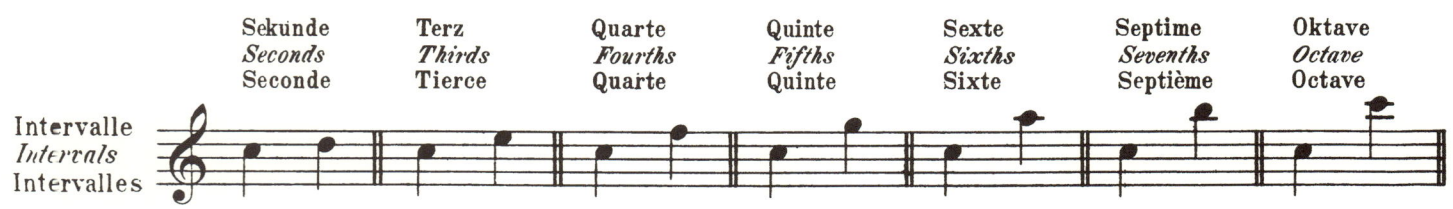

Geltung der Noten und der Pausen	Value of the Notes and Rests	Valeur des Notes et des Silences

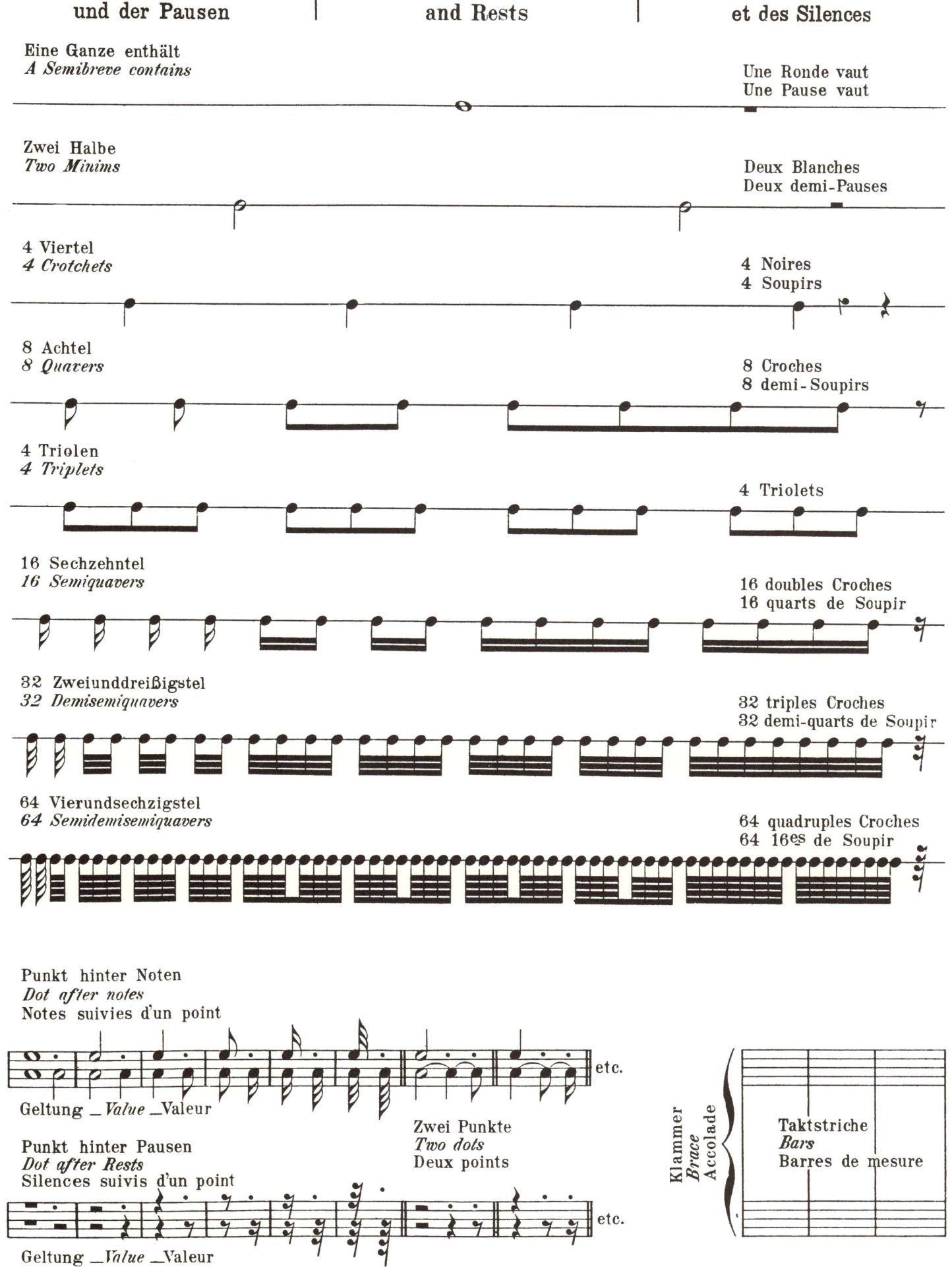

C Viervierteltakt	**C** *Common time*	**C** Mesure à 4 temps
2/4 Zweivierteltakt	2/4 *Two-four time*	2/4 Mesure à 2 quatre
3/4 Dreivierteltakt	3/4 *Three-four time*	3/4 Mesure à 3 quatre
6/8 Sechsachteltakt	6/8 *Six-eight time*	6/8 Mesure à 6 huit
3/8 Dreiachteltakt	3/8 *Three-eight time*	3/8 Mesure à 3 huit
9/8 Neunachteltakt	9/8 *Nine-eight time*	9/8 Mesure à 9 huit

Versetzungszeichen	**Accidentals**	**Signes altératifs**
♯ = Kreuz	♯ *Sharp*	♯ Dièse
♭ = Bee	♭ *Flat*	♭ Bémol
♮ = Auflösungszeichen (Widerrufungszeichen)	♮ *Natural*	♮ Bécarre

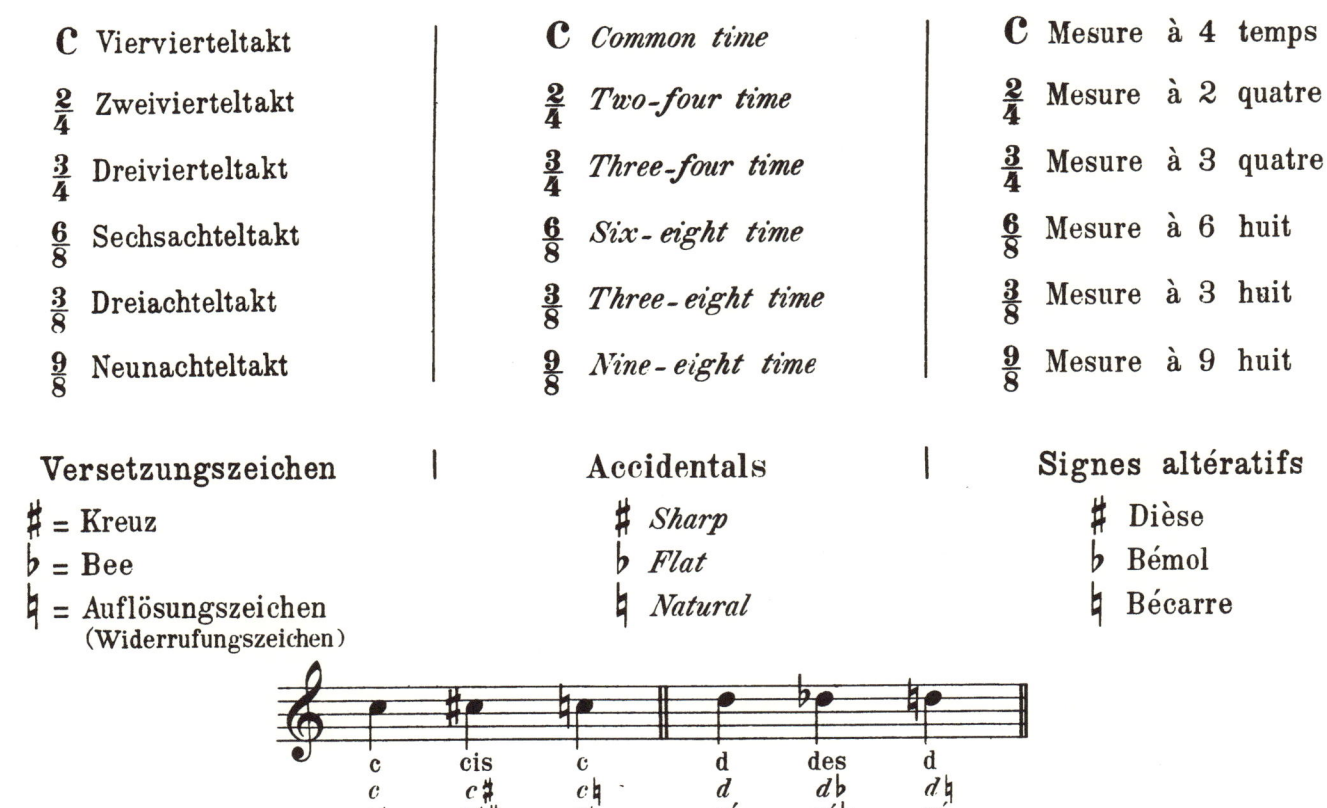

Namen der Noten mit ♯
Names of the notes with ♯
Noms des notes diésées

Namen der Noten mit ♭
Names of the notes with ♭
Noms des notes bémolisées

Chromatisch
Chromatic
Chromatique

Enharmonisch
Enharmonic
Enharmonique

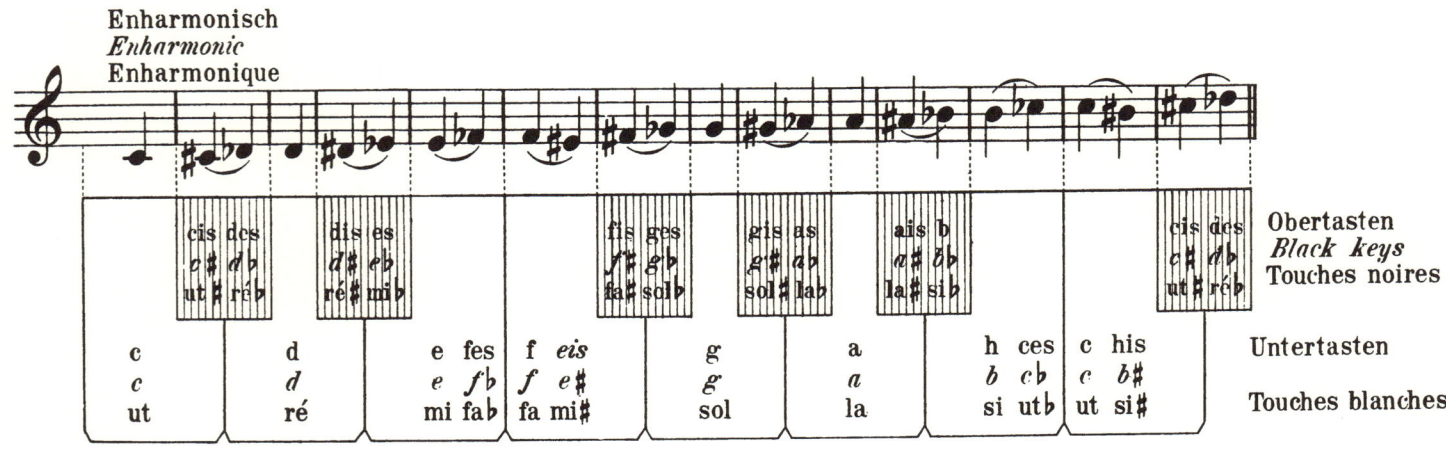

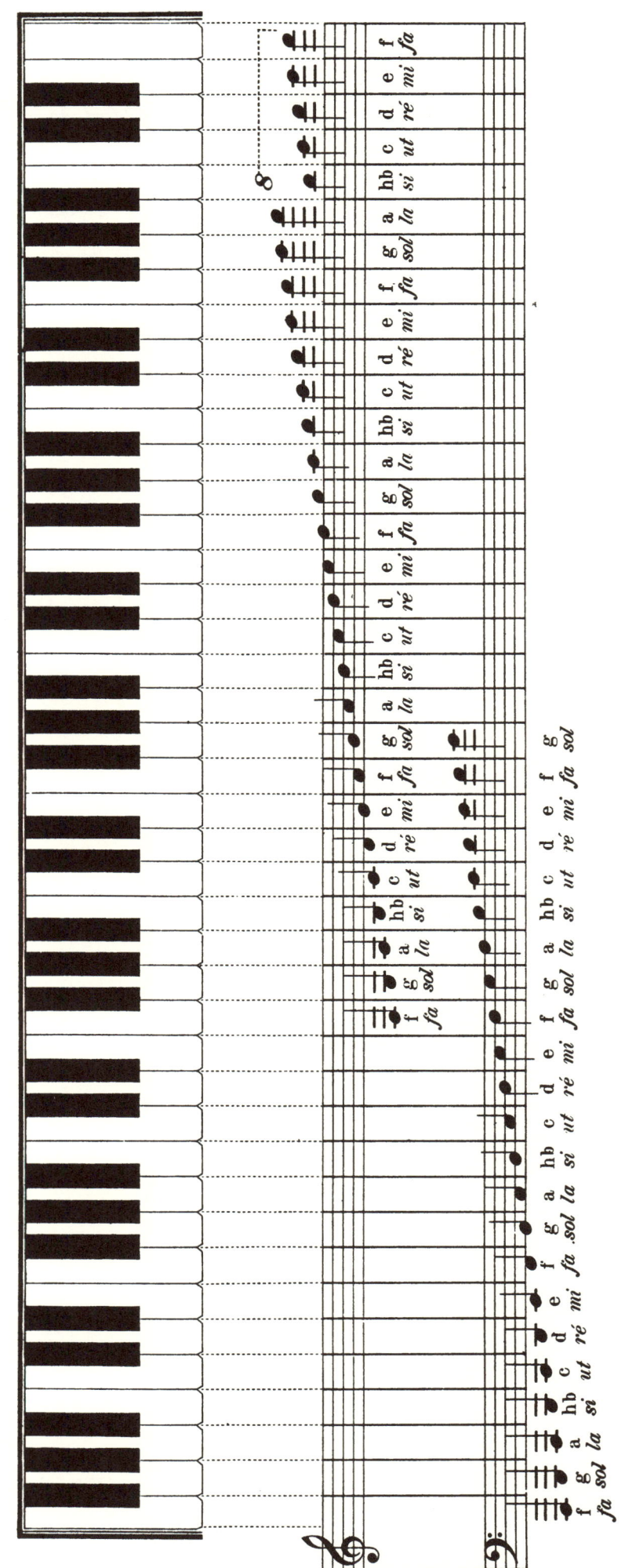

Abbildung der Klaviatur von 6 Oktaven

Keyboard of the Piano with 6 Octaves | Tableau du Clavier à six Octaves

8

Übungen im Anschlage der Finger der rechten Hand

Jeder Finger muß genau in dem Augenblicke aufgehoben werden, in welchem der nächstfolgende anschlägt.

Die Bewegung der Finger muß gleichmäßig, bestimmt und anfangs langsam geschehen.

Der Anschlag darf nicht zu stark sein, damit die Hand und die Finger sich nicht jene krampfhafte Anspannung der Muskeln angewöhnen, welche ein schwerfälliges Spiel erzeugen.

Jede Nummer muß so oft wiederholt werden, bis der Lehrer zufrieden ist

Exercises in Touch for the Right Hand

Each finger must be lifted up at the exact moment when the next finger strikes the key.

The movement of the fingers must be even, firm and, at the beginning, slow.

The touch should not be too strong, else the muscles of the hand and fingers will acquire a cramped tension which will result in a hard and heavy style of playing.

Each exercise must be repeated as often as the master requires

Exercices pour les doigts de la main droite seule

Il faut relever chaque doigt au moment même où le suivant attaque une autre touche.

Le mouvement des doigts s'opérera très également, avec précision et d'abord lentement.

Le toucher ne doit pas être trop fort, afin que la main et les doigts ne s'habituent pas à contracter une sorte de crispation, nerveuse qui occasionnerait une exécution lourde.

Chaque numéro doit être répété jusqu'à ce que le professeur soit complètement satisfait

Übungen im Anschlage der Finger der linken Hand

Exercises in Touch for the Left Hand

Exercices pour les doigts de la main gauche seule

033

Übungen im Zusammenspielen der beiden Hände | Exercises for Both Hands Together | Exercices pour les deux mains ensemble

Anmerkung

Die Übungen dieser beiden Seiten spielt der Schüler (nach Anleitung des Lehrers) anfangs auswendig. Wenn derselbe sich die wenigen nötigen Kenntnisse für die folgenden Stücke angeeignet hat, so kann man schon während dieser Anschlagsübungen mit den folgenden Seiten beginnen. Weitern Stoff zu Fingerübungen (welche anfangs auch auswendig gespielt werden können) findet man am Schlusse dieser Vorschule im Anhang

Note

The exercises on these two pages should first be played from memory under the direction of the master. When the pupil has acquired the necessary knowledge for the following pieces, he may proceed to them while still practising these exercises on touch. The appendix contains further exercises on touch, which should also at first be played from memory

Remarque

L'élève jouera tout d'abord ces deux pages par coeur en suivant les indications du professeur. Quand il aura acquis les connaissances indispensables pour les morceaux suivants, on pourra commencer les pages suivantes pendant les exercices de toucher. On trouvera au supplément d'autres exercices de doigté qu'on pourra également jouer d'abord par coeur

Dreihändig
Der Lehrer

For Three Hands
The master

À trois mains
Le maître

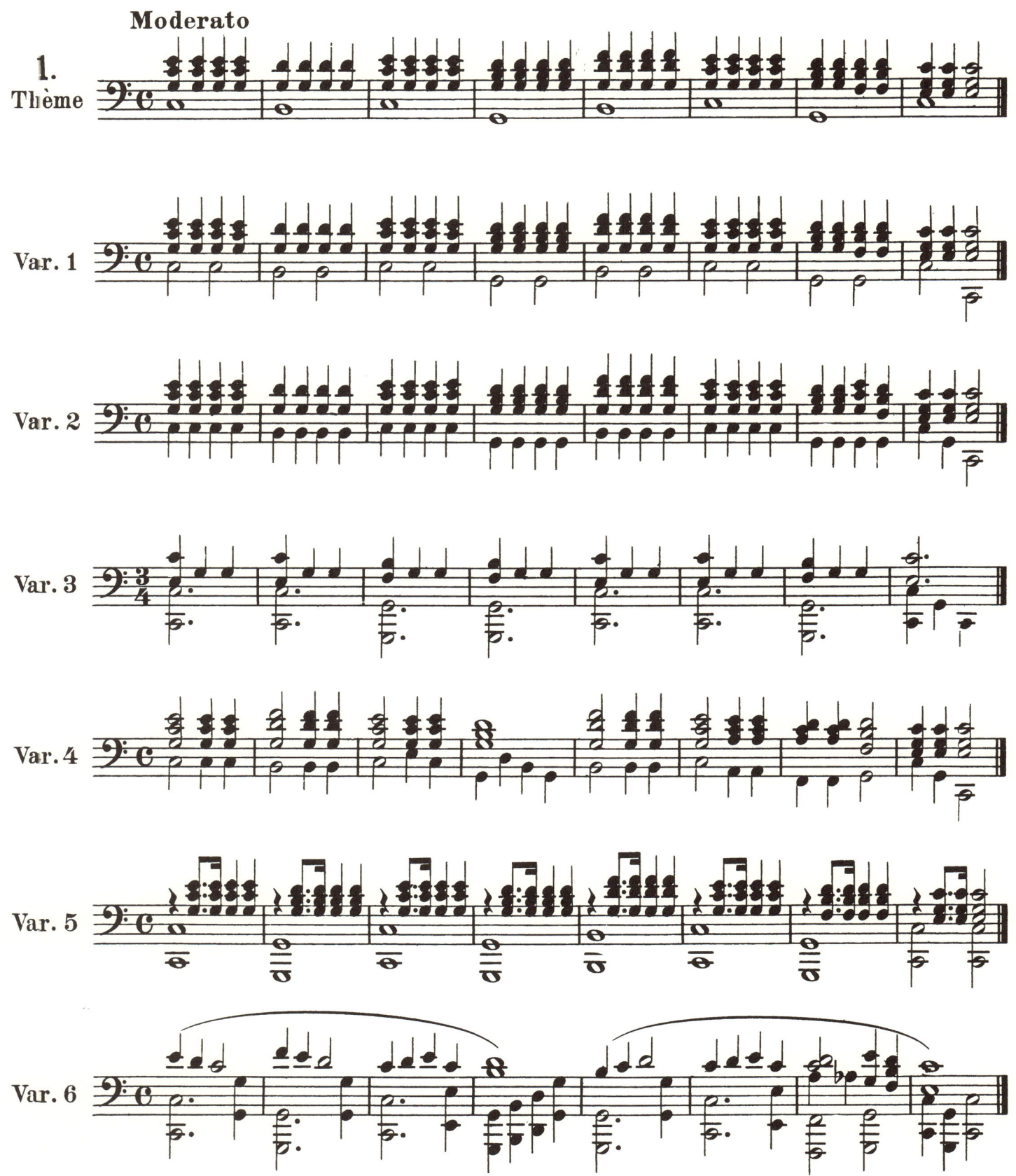

Dreihändig	For Three Hands	À trois mains
Der Schüler	*The Pupil*	L'élève
Für die rechte Hand allein	*For the right hand alone*	Pour la main droite seule
	Position of the hand	

Handlage  Position de la main

1.
Aufgabe
Thema
Theme
Thème

Tempo Moderato (Mäßige Bewegung – *Moderate time* – Mouvement modéré)

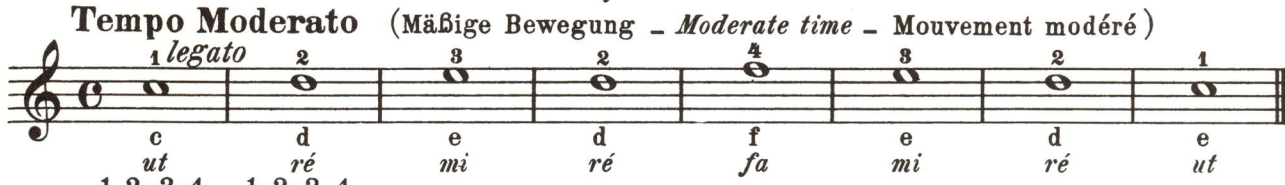

Der Schüler muß anfangs laut dazu zählen
At first the pupil must count aloud
L'élève doit compter d'abord tout haut

Slur: legato, connected, gliding

Schleifbogen: legato, gebunden, geschleift    Liaison

| Die Töne sollen miteinander verbunden werden. Dies geschieht, wenn der Finger, welcher auf der Taste liegt, dieselbe nicht eher wieder verläßt, als bis der folgende niederfällt. In der Regel soll man immer so spielen. Wenn eine Taste zweimal oder öfter mit demselben Finger anzuschlagen ist, so muß man die Hand in die Höhe heben | *The notes must be played connectedly. This is done by letting each finger remain on the key until the next finger strikes. This style of playing should always be adopted as a rule. If the same key is to be struck twice or oftener by the same finger, the hand must be lifted up* | Les sons doivent être liés ensemble; ceci a lieu lorsque le doigt qui est sur la touche ne la quitte pas avant que le suivant n'en frappe une autre. En règle générale, on doit toujours jouer ainsi. Si l'on doit attaquer deux ou plusieurs fois de suite la même note avec le même doigt, il faut relever la main |

Variation (Veränderung)

Var. 1

Var. 2

Var. 3

Var. 4

Var. 5

Var. 6

Lehrer

Schüler

Rests or pauses

Pausen
Schweigezeichen — *Silences*

Während der Dauer einer Pause darf der Finger nicht auf der Taste liegen bleiben und die Hand muß sich heben	*During the value of a rest, the finger should not rest on the key, and the hand must be lifted up*	Le doigt ne reste jamais sur la touche pendant la durée d'un silence et il faut relever la main

Lehrer

Schüler

Dreihändig	For Three Hands	À trois mains
Für die linke Hand allein	*For the left hand alone*	Pour la main gauche seule

16

Lehrer

8033

Schüler

Repeats

Wiederholungszeichen ‖: :‖ Reprises

Var. 5

Var. 6

Position of the hands

Handlage — Position de la main

g   a   hb   c   d

sol   la   si   ut   ré

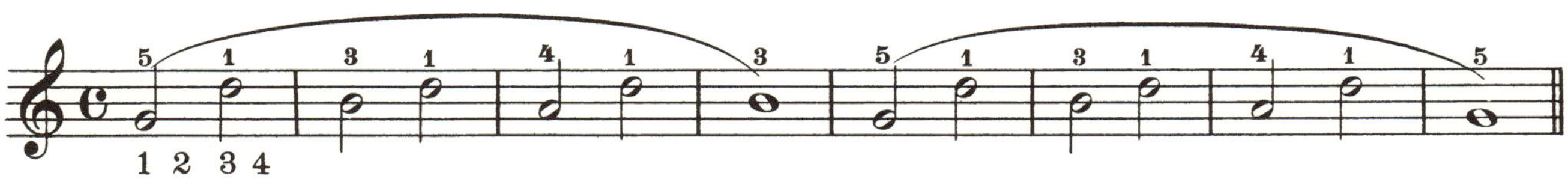

Var. 7

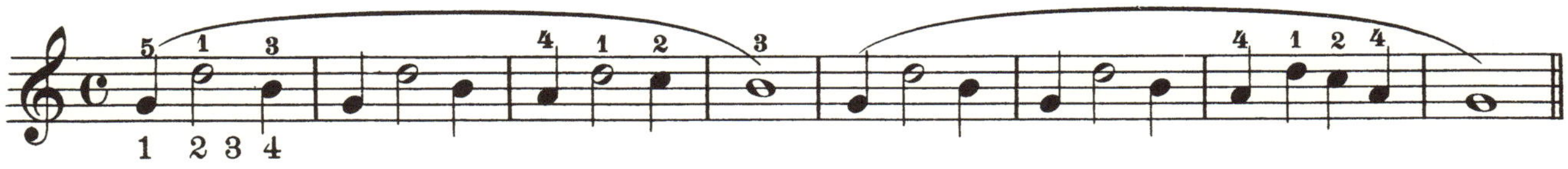

Var. 8

Seconda

Vierhändig | For four hands | A quatre mains

Prima

(Die erste, obere Stimme) | *(The treble part)* | (La premiere partie)

1 2 3 4 5
c d e f g
ut ré mi fa sol

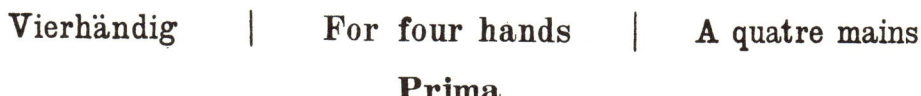

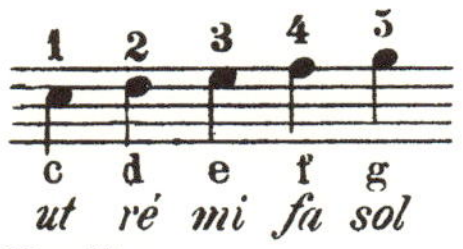

Handlagen
Positions of the hands
Positions des mains

5 4 3 2 1
c d e f g
ut ré mi fa sol

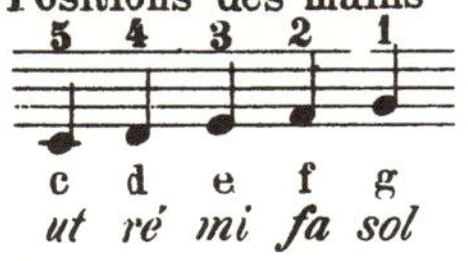

Jede Taste behält den ihr in den Handlagen vorgeschriebenen Finger

Each finger retains this positi

Chaque touche conserve le doigt prescrit dans les positions des mains

Moderato

3.

Rechte Hand
Right hand
Main droite
Linke Hand
Left hand
Main gauche

4.

5.

6.

7.

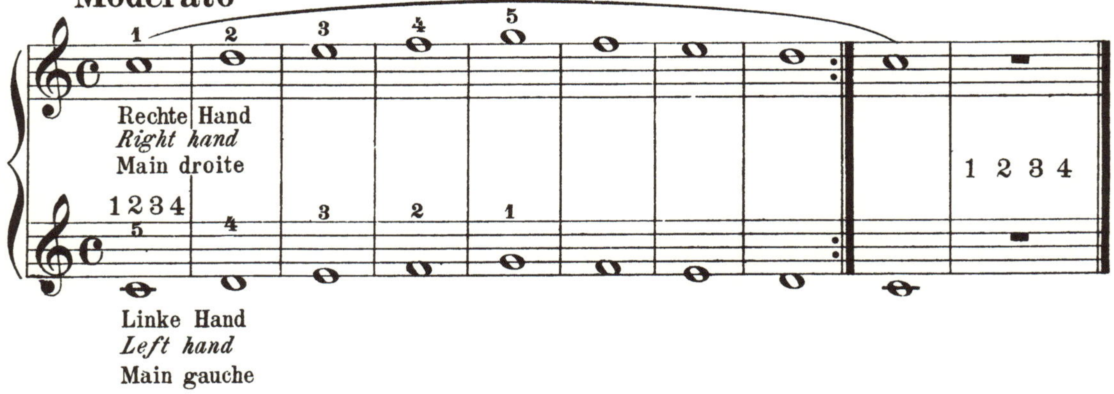

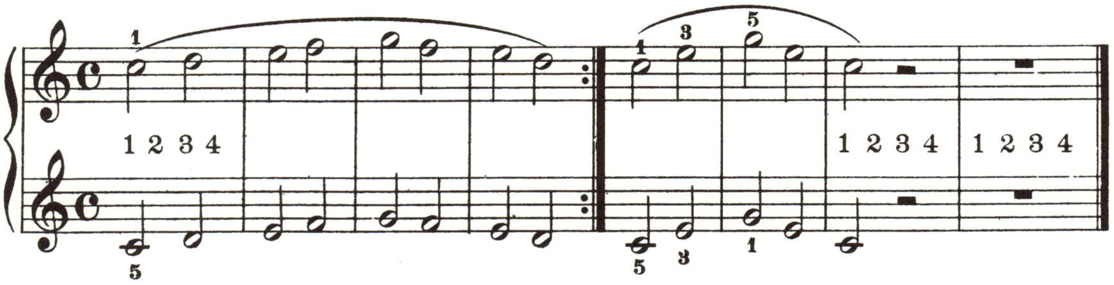

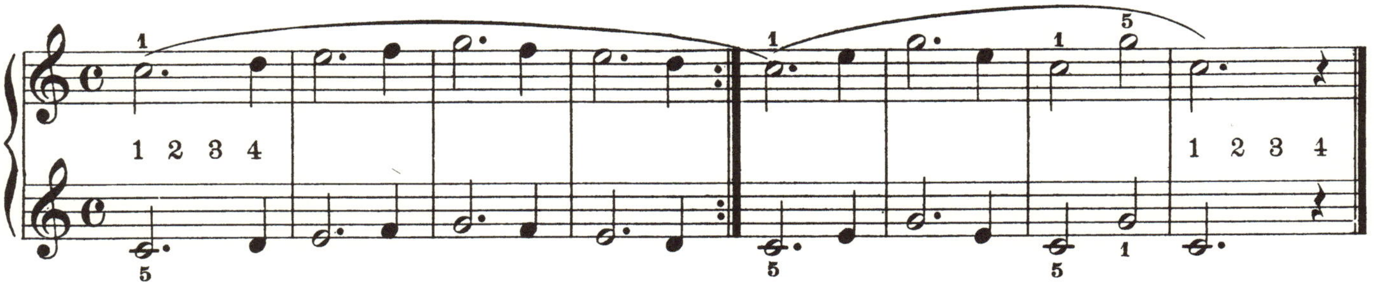

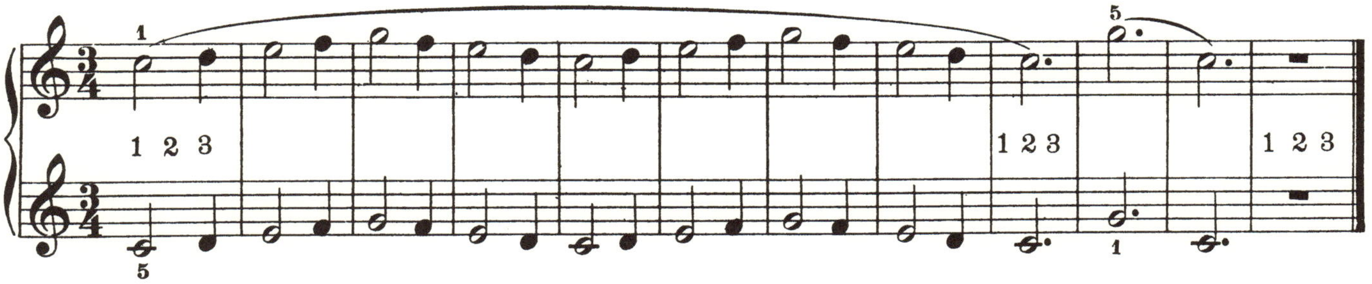

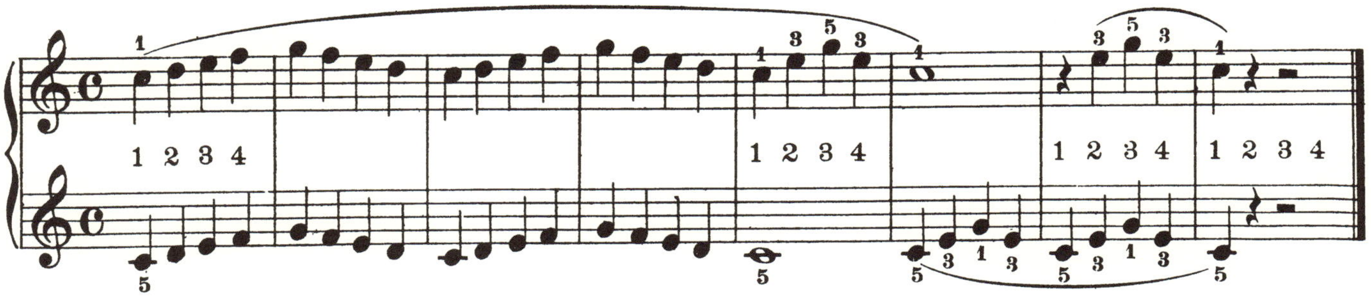

Seconda

8.

Allegretto

9.

Prima

Prima

Zweihändige Übungsstücke

Der Schüler vergesse nicht, daß gute Haltung des Körpers, der Arme, der Hände und der Finger, sowie guter Anschlag und strenges Takthalten die Grundlagen eines guten Spieles sind

Exercises for Both Hands

The pupil should never forget that a good attitude of the body, arms hands and fingers, together with a good touch and strict time-keeping, are the foundation of a good style

Exercices à deux mains

L'Élève ne doit jamais oublier qu'une bonne position du corps, des bras, des mains et des doigts, ainsi qu'un bon toucher et une grande précision dans la mesure sont la base d'une bonne exécution

Tie. *Two notes on the same degree*

Bindebogen   Liaison sur deux notes pareilles

Die 2te Note darf nicht wieder ange- | *The second note is not to be repeat-* | Il ne faut pas que la seconde note
schlagen werden; der Finger muß a - | *ed, but during its value the finger* | soit répétée. Le doigt devra rester sur
ber während der Dauer dieser Note auf | *must remain upon the key* | la touche pendant la durée de cette note
der Taste liegen bleiben

legato

Seconda

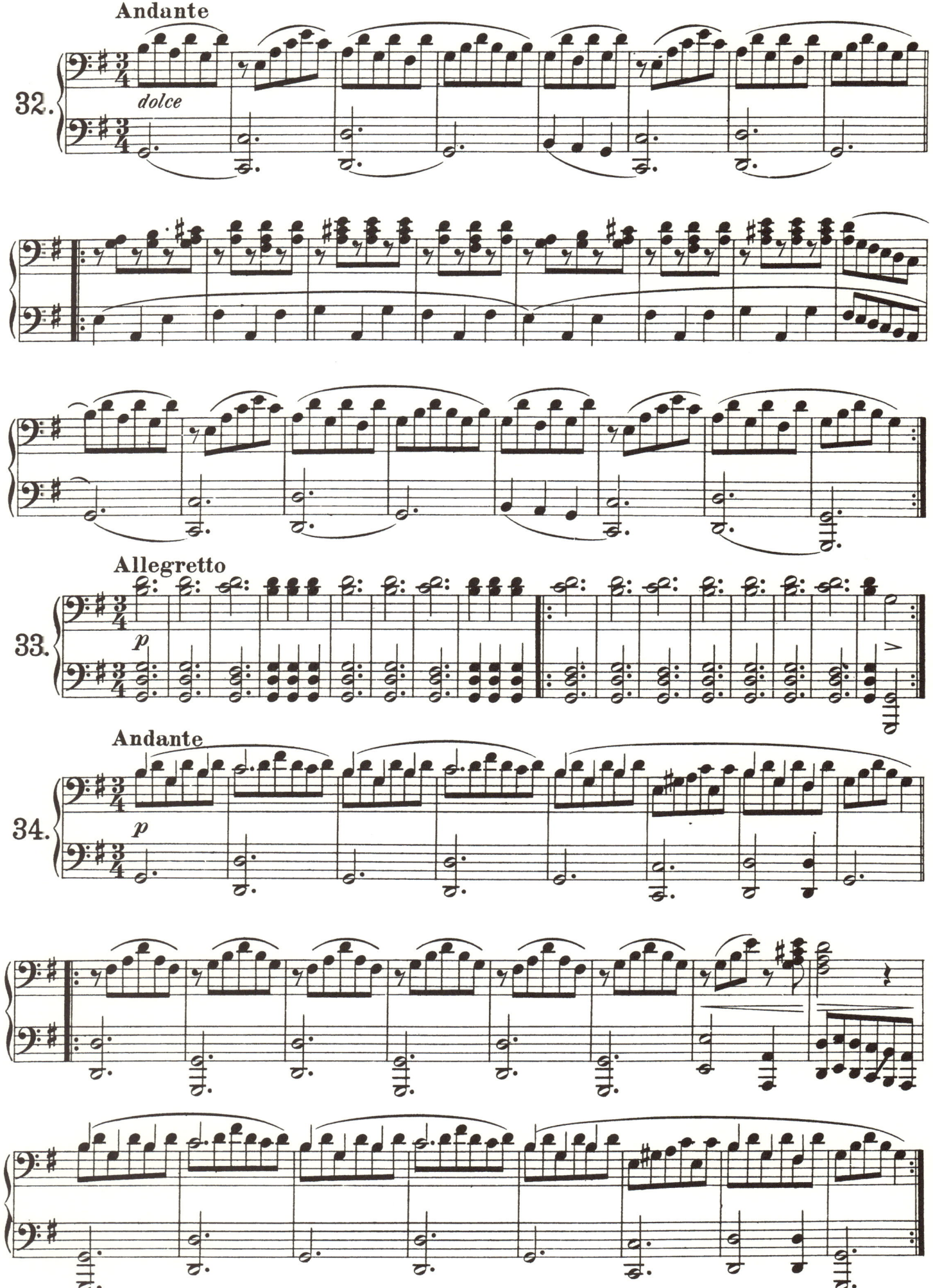

Prima

Seconda

Seconda

Moderato

44.

8‑‑‑‑‑‑Octava

Die Noten, über denen dieses Zeichen steht, und soweit das‑‑‑‑‑‑ geht, müssen eine Oktave höher gespielt werden

8‑‑‑‑‑‑Octave

Notes with this mark above them must be played an octave higher as far as the‑‑‑‑‑‑extends

8‑‑‑‑‑‑à l'octave

Les notes surmontées du signe *8va* doivent être exécutées une octave plus haut jusqu'à la fin de la ligne‑‑‑‑‑‑

Beispiel / *Example* / Exemple

wird so gespielt: / *played:* / Exécution:

Prima

Moderato

44.

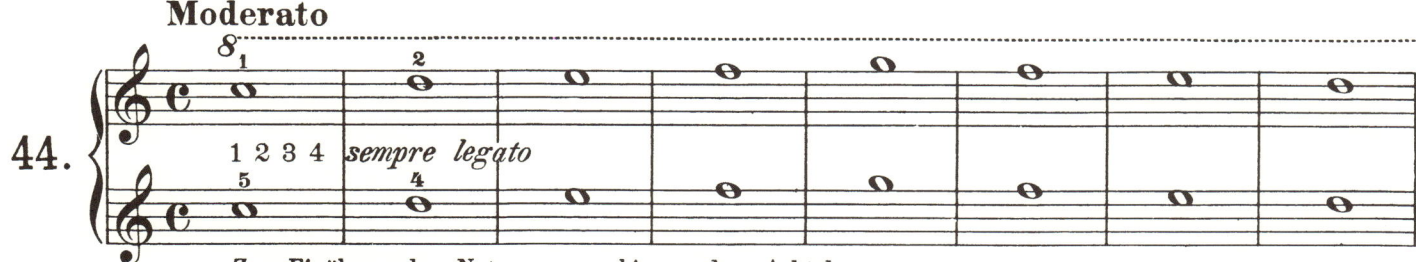

Zur Einübung des Notenwertes bis zu den Achteln
To practise the value of the notes up to quavers
Pour étudier la valeur des notes jusqu'aux croches

38

Übung in Achteln | Exercise in quavers | Exercice en Chroches

Moderato

45.

Comodo

46.

1ma *) Zum ersten Male wird dieser Takt gespielt
This bar to be played to be played the first time
à jouer à la 1re fois

2da *) Zum zweiten Male dieser statt jenem
This bar the second time instead of the other
à jouer à la 2me fois

*)1ma＝prima volta zum ersten Male   *)1ma＝*the first time*   *)1ma＝pour la première fois
2da＝seconda volta zum zweiten Male   2da＝*the second time*   2da＝pour la seconde fois

Comodo

Die Ellenbogen dürfen nicht vom Kör- per abstehen, wenn auch die Hände we_ter auseinander zu liegen kommen	*The elbows must not project from the body, even when the hands have to play far apart*	Les coudes ne doivent pas s'élo- igner du corps, lors même que les mains s'écartent

NB. Zur Vergleichung der Noten des G-Schlüssels und derjenigen des F-Schlüssels, welche auf gleichen Tasten gespielt werden
NB. To serve as a comparison of the notes of the treble and the bass clef, wich are played on the same keys
NB. Pour comparer les notes de la clef de sol et celles de la clef de fa qui doivent se jouer sur les mêmes touches

Moderato

Moderato

55.

mf

legato

mf (mezzo forte) halbstark — *half loud* — demi-forte

Allegretto

56.

f

Allegretto

57.

f

p (piano) leise — *softly* — doux

≤ zunehmend — *increasing in loudness* — en augmentant
≥ abnehmend — *decreasing in loudness* — en diminuant

♩ Die Note hervorgehoben — ♩ *Accent the Note* — ♩ Il faut accentuer la note

60. Comodo

cresc.(crescendo) zunehmend — *increasing in loudness* — en augmentant
dim.(diminuendo) abnehmend — *decreasing in loudness* — en diminuant

Allegro moderato mäßig schnell
moderately fast
vif, modéré

61.

dolce

legato

dolce sanft — *softly* — doux

Allegro moderato

62.

(musical notation)

Wenn ein Punkt über einer Note steht, so muß dieselbe abgestoßen werden; dies geschieht, wenn man gleich nach dem Anschlage die Taste wieder verläßt	*A note with a dot over it must be sharply detached. This is done by letting the key go immediately after striking it*	Lorsqu'un point se trouve sur une note, il faut la détacher vivement; cela se fait en retirant le doigt d'une touche aussitôt après l'avoir frappee

Beispiel:
Example:
Exemple:

wird so gespielt:
Played:
Exécution:

Beispiel: / *Example:* / Exemple: — wird so gespielt: / *Played:* / Exécution:

48

Übungen in Doppelgriffen | Exercises on Double Notes | Exercices en doubles notes

Rechte Hand allein / Right hand alone / Main droite seule

Linke Hand allein / Left hand alone / Main gauche seule

Jede Übung wenigstens 4 mal
Repeat 4 times at least
Chaque exercice au moins 4 fois

Allegretto

66. *dolce* *legato*

Moderato

67. *mf*

NB. Das Handgelenk darf ja nicht steif gehalten werden
NB. The wrist must not on any account be held stiffly
NB. Le poignet ne doit jamais contracter de raideur

50

Der Schüler bemühe sich die beiden Töne der Terzen zu gleicher
Zeit hören zu lassen und spiele
streng legato

*The pupil should endeavour to
sound both notes of the thirds
together, and play strictly legato*

L'élève s'efforcera de faire en -
tendre en même temps les deux
notes des tierces et devra les jouer
rigoureusement legato (liées)

Tonleiter in G dur | Scale of G major | Gamme en sol majeur

Vorzeichnung
Key signature
Armature

71.

72. **Comodo**
dolce
legato

73. **Moderato**
dolce

Zufällige Versetzungszeichen
Accidentals
Altérations accidentelles

Triolen | Triplets | Triolets

Tonleiter in D dur | Scale of D major | Gamme en ré majeur

Moderato

75.

Allegro moderato

76.

Lockeres Handgelenk | *Loose wrist* | Articulation libre du poignet

Tonleiter in A dur | Scale of A major | Gamme en la majeur

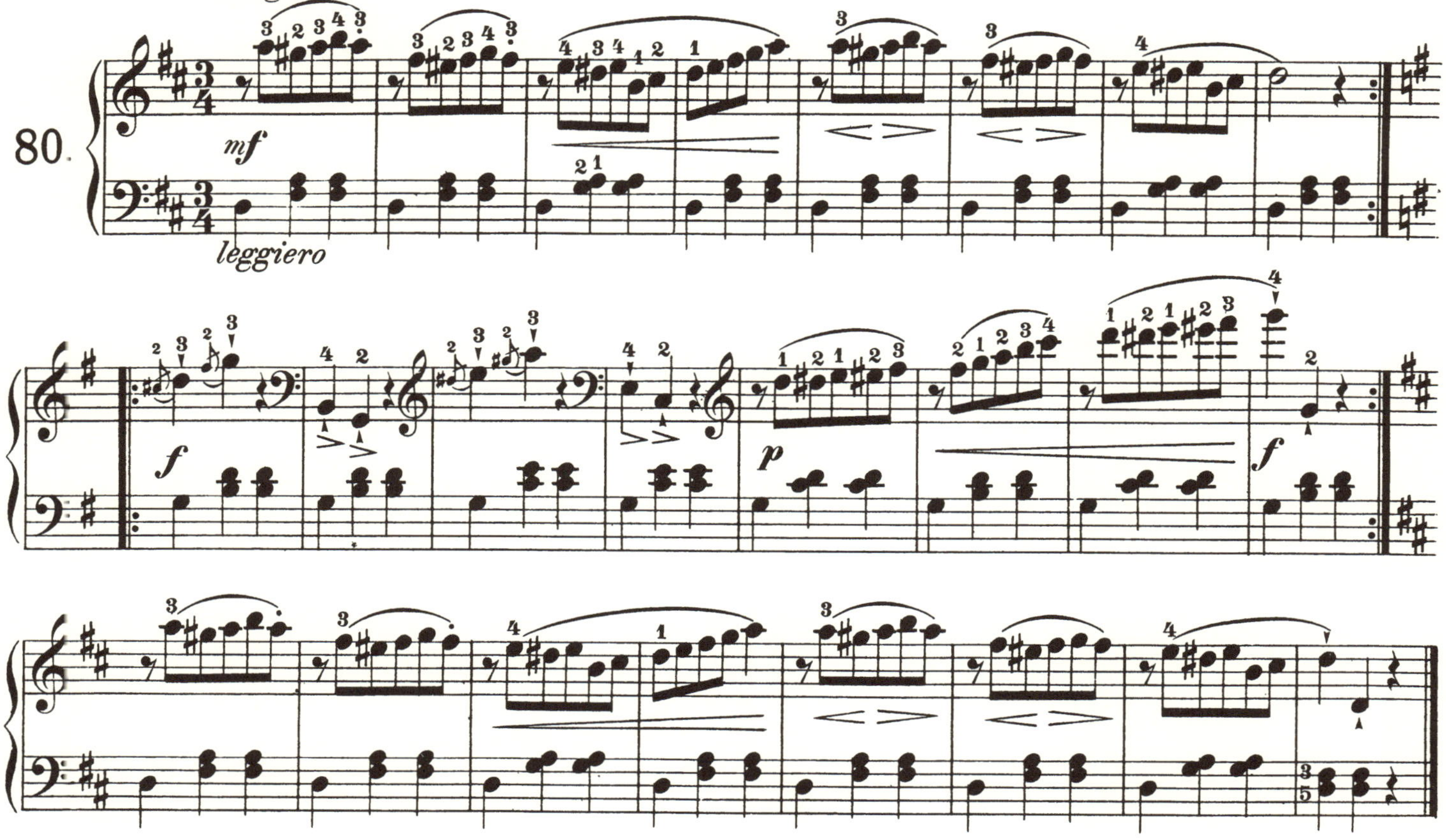

Vorschlag
Appoggiatura
Appoggiature

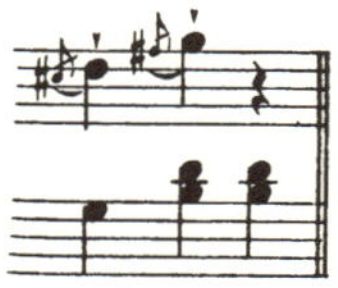

Ausführung
Played
Exécution

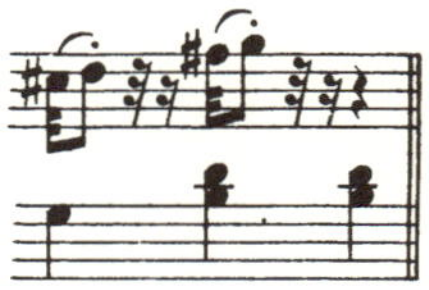

NB. Wenn die Note nach dem Vorschlage keinen Punkt über sich hat, so muß sie nach ihrem Werte ausgehalten werden

N.B. If the note after the appoggiatura has no dot upon it, it must be sustained during its full value

NB. Quand il n'y a pas de point sur une note après l'appoggiature, il faut lui donner toute sa valeur

Tonleiter in E-dur | Scale of E major | Gamme en mi majeur

Allegretto

84.

85.

⌢ **Halt, Ruhezeichen**
Die Note soll wenigstens noch einmal
so lange ausgehalten werden

⌢ *Pause*
The note must be sustained at
least as long again

⌢ Point d'orgue
La note doit se soutenir au moins
le double de sa valeur

marcato (hervorgehoben — *emphasized* — marqué)

Seconda

Prima

| Zur Einübung des Notenwertes bis zu Sechzehnteln | For practising the values of the notes up to semiquavers | Pour étudier la valeur des notes jusqu' aux doubles croches |

Moderato

staccato (abgestoßen) — *detached* — détaché

| Zur Beförderung der Geläufigkeit | To facilitate fluency | Pour développer l'agilité |

Allegro moderato

62

8033

Tonleiter in A moll | Scale of A minor | Gamme en la mineur

Allegretto

91.

Tonleiter in F dur | Scale of F major | Gamme en Fa majeur

Allegro moderato

Allegretto

94.

Allegretto

95.

Allegro (munter *vif*)

96.

97. Allegretto

98. Allegro

∧ Die Note mit diesem Zeichen soll stark hervorgehoben werden | ∧ *Notes with this mark must be strongly accentuated* | La note sur laquelle se trouve le signe ∧ doit être fortement accentuée

B Dur | B♭ major | Si Bémol majeur

99. Adagio (langsam *slowly* lent)

dolce

legato

Allegro moderato

101.

Moderato

102.

dolce

legato

cresc.

f

dim.

p

p

cre — *scen* — — *do*

p

cre — *scen* — — *do*

f

Der Fingerwechsel, ohne die Taste wieder anzuschlagen, muß sehr schnell geschehen
The change of finger must be done very quickly without striking the key again
Le changement de doigts sans refrapper la touche devra se faire très rapidement

Allegro moderato

103.

Allegretto

104.

Chromatische Tonleiter | Chromatic Scale | Gamme Chromatique

Rechte Hand allein
Right hand alone
Main droite seule

I

Dieser Fingersatz ist für kleine Hände der bequemste
This fingering is the easiest for small hands
Ce doigté est le plus commode pour les petites mains

Rechte Hand allein
Right hand alone
Main droite seule

II

Dieser Fingersatz ist der gebräuchlichste
This is usual fingering
Ce doigté est le plus usité

Linke Hand allein
Left hand alone
Main gauche seule

III

Dieser Fingersatz ist für kleine Hände der bequemste
This fingering is the easiest for small hands
Ce doigté est le plus commode pour les petites mains

Linke Hand allein
Left hand alone
Main gauche seule

IV

Dieser Fingersatz ist der gebräuchlichste
This is usual fingering
Ce doigté est le plus usité

Rechte Hand allein
Right hand alone
Main droite seule

V

Linke Hand allein
Left hand alone
Main gauche seule

VI

VII

Anhang

Fingerübungen, welche in die Vorschule einzuschalten und gehörig einzuüben sind

Für die rechte Hand allein

Jede Nummer wird einigemàle wiederholt. Man kann dieselben durch zwei Oktaven ausdehnen

Appendix

Finger exercises which may be intercalated into the Instruction Book, and must be thoroughly practised

For the Right Hand alone

Each exercise must be repeated several times. The exercises may also be extended to two octaves

Supplément

Exercices de doigté à intercaler dans la méthode préparatoire et qu'il faut bien étudier

Pour la main droite seule

Chaque numéro devra se répéter plusieurs fois. On pourra le jouer dans l'étendue de deux octaves

Für die linke Hand allein | For the left hand alone | Pour la main gauche seule

Für beide Hände zusammen | For Both Hands Together | Pour les deux mains ensemble

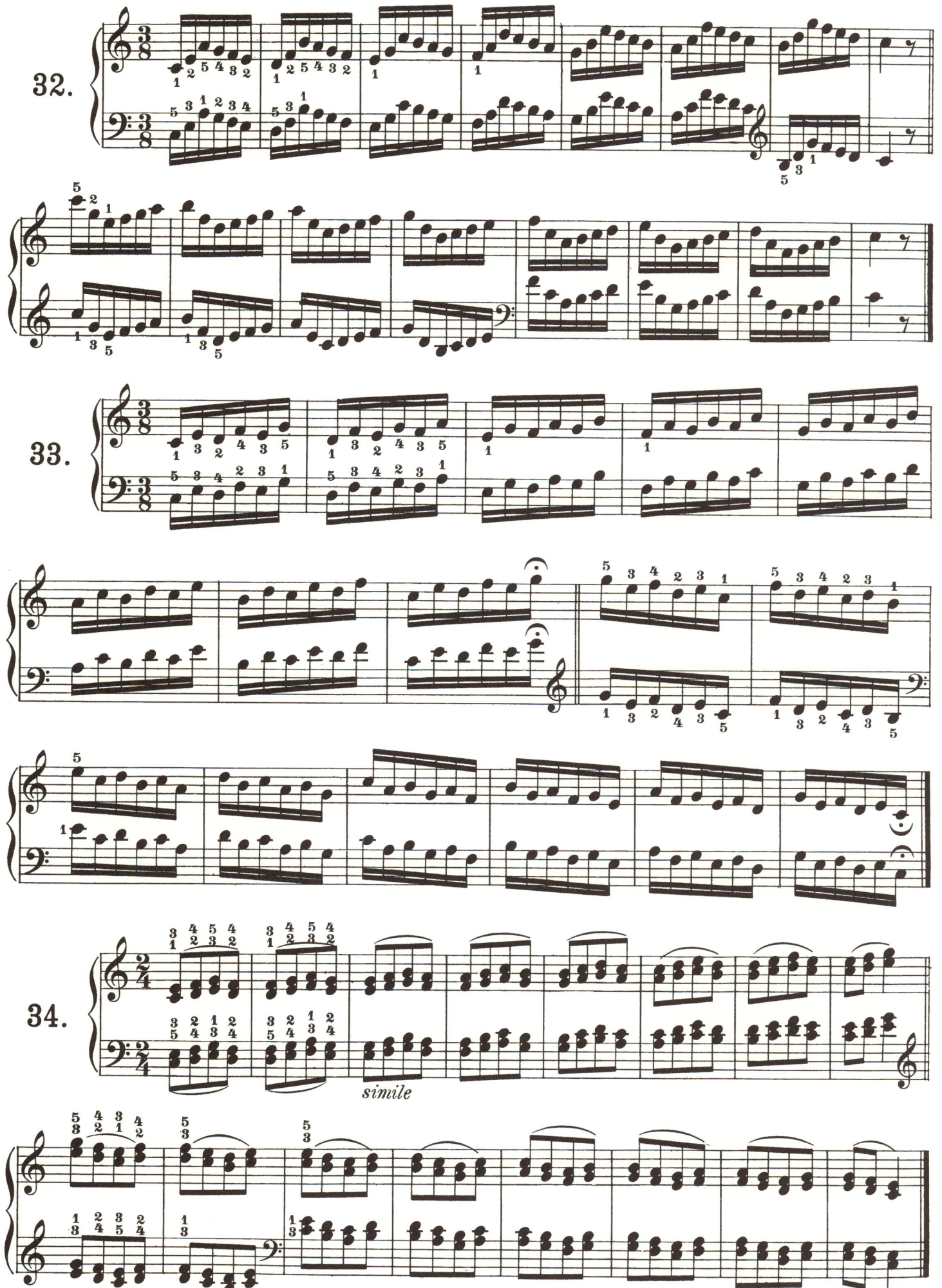

24 Dur-und Moll- tonleitern

geordnet nach der Ähnlichkeit des Fingersatzes und zur Vergleichung von Dur und Moll

24 Major and Minor Scales

arranged according to the similarity of their fingering and for the comparison of major and minor

24 Gammes en Tons Majeurs et Mineurs

disposées selon la ressemblance du doigté et pour la comparaison des tons majeurs et mineurs

1. C dur _ *C major* _ Ut majeur

6. D moll _ *D minor* _ Ré mineur

2. C moll _ *C minor* _ Ut mineur

7. A dur _ *A major* _ La majeur

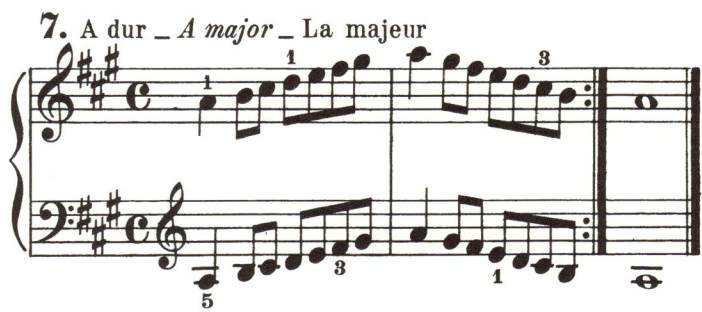

3. G dur _ *G major* _ Sol majeur

8. A moll _ *A minor* _ La mineur

4. G moll _ *G minor* _ Sol mineur

9. E dur _ *E major* _ Mi majeur

5. D dur _ *D major* _ Ré majeur

10. E moll _ *E minor* _ Mi mineur

85

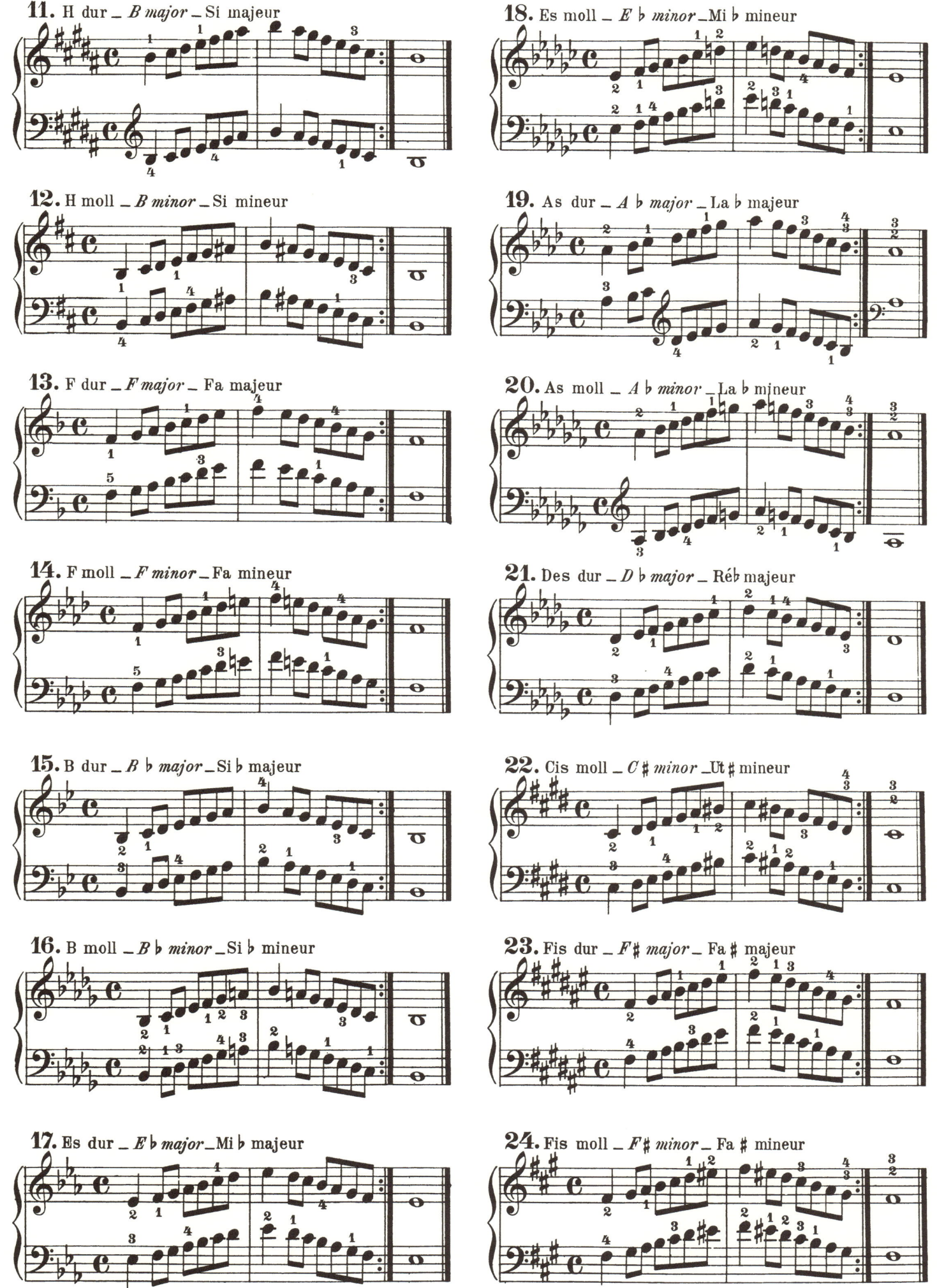

11. H dur _ B major _ Si majeur

12. H moll _ B minor _ Si mineur

13. F dur _ F major _ Fa majeur

14. F moll _ F minor _ Fa mineur

15. B dur _ B♭ major _ Si♭ majeur

16. B moll _ B♭ minor _ Si♭ mineur

17. Es dur _ E♭ major _ Mi♭ majeur

18. Es moll _ E♭ minor _ Mi♭ mineur

19. As dur _ A♭ major _ La♭ majeur

20. As moll _ A♭ minor _ La♭ mineur

21. Des dur _ D♭ major _ Ré♭ majeur

22. Cis moll _ C♯ minor _ Ut♯ mineur

23. Fis dur _ F♯ major _ Fa♯ majeur

24. Fis moll _ F♯ minor _ Fa♯ mineur

8033

Außer den vorhergehenden Moll-tonleitern sind noch folgende 2 Arten derselben im Gebrauche	*In addition to the above minor scales the following two are in use*	Indépendamment de ces gammes mineures, il y a encore deux autres manières de les faire

Reihenfolge aller Tonarten und ihrer Verwandtschaften	All the Keys in their relative Positions	Ordre de tous les tons et de leurs Relations

C dur	A moll	G dur	E moll	D dur	H moll
C major	*A minor*	*G major*	*E minor*	*D major*	*B minor*
Ut majeur	La mineur	Sol majeur	Mi mineur	Ré majeur	Si mineur

A dur	Fis moll	E dur	Cis moll	H dur	Gis moll
A major	*F♯ minor*	*E major*	*C♯ minor*	*B major*	*G♯ minor*
La majeur	Fa ♯ mineur	Mi majeur	Ut ♯ mineur	Si majeur	Sol ♯ mineur

Fis dur	Dis moll	Cis dur	Ais moll	F dur	D moll
F♯ major	*D♯ minor*	*C♯ major*	*A♯ minor*	*F major*	*D minor*
Fa ♯ majeur	Ré ♯ mineur	Ut ♯ majeur	La ♯ mineur	Fa majeur	Ré mineur

B dur	G moll	Es dur	C moll	As dur	F moll
B♭ major	*G minor*	*E♭ major*	*C minor*	*A♭ major*	*F minor*
Si ♭ majeur	Sol mineur	Mi ♭ majeur	Ut mineur	La ♭ majeur	Fa mineur

Des dur	B moll	Ges dur	Es moll	Ces dur	As moll
D♭ major	*B♭ minor*	*G♭ major*	*E♭ minor*	*C♭ major*	*A♭ minor*
Ré ♭ majeur	Si ♭ mineur	Sol ♭ majeur	Mi ♭ mineur	Ut ♭ majeur	La ♭ mineur

Fine